What people are saying about …

When You Lose Someone You Love

"Written in Richard Exley's inimitably compassionate style, this book goes right to the heart of the person struggling with the pain of loss. Written in the form of letters to a grief-stricken friend, Exley combines his personal journey through sorrow with Scripture, poetry, and empathetic advice. I cannot count the number of copies I have given, nor can I begin to recall all the stories from people who have found comfort and hope in these pages. This book is a must-read for those who are coping with the morass of sorrow, as well as for those who are ministering comfort to the grieving."

Evelyn H. Looper, counselor,
educator, and minister

"I have known Richard Exley personally for over a decade and do not know of another person who oozes with the compassionate love of God more than he. Richard lives to comfort others, and his writings certainly reflect that fact."

Max Davis, author of *Luke's Passage*
and *Desperate Dependence*

"Richard Exley is the caring friend and pastor who, through his book *When You Lose Someone You Love,* brings hope, help, and encouragement to grieving individuals. This book is my preferred ministry resource for helping families who are facing such great loss, and it is also my textbook for training Bible-college students in pastoral care."

Rev. Thomas Harrison, church consultant and America's Secret Church Shopper, Tulsa, Oklahoma

Presented to

Debbie Millner

No pain is greater than that which you experience following the death of someone you love. So often you are isolated with your sorrow. No one seems to understand what you are experiencing, and those who do are often at a loss for words. Quite frequently you are separated by long distances from those who would love and support you in your time of loss.

Please accept this small book, not as a substitute for our presence, but as an expression of our deepest love and continuing concern for you in your time of grief.

From

Karen B Gross

Jan. 2013

when
you lose
someone
you love

comfort for
those who grieve

richard exley

David C Cook®
transforming lives together

WHEN YOU LOSE SOMEONE YOU LOVE
Published by David C. Cook
4050 Lee Vance View
Colorado Springs, CO 80918 U.S.A.

David C. Cook Distribution Canada
55 Woodslee Avenue, Paris, Ontario, Canada N3L 3E5

David C. Cook U.K., Kingsway Communications
Eastbourne, East Sussex BN23 6NT, England

David C. Cook and the graphic circle C logo
are registered trademarks of Cook Communications Ministries.

The Web site addresses recommended throughout this book
are offered as a resource to you. These Web sites are not
intended in any way to be or imply an endorsement on the part
of David C. Cook, nor do we vouch for their content.

All Scripture quotations, unless otherwise noted, are taken from the
Holy Bible, New International Version®. *NIV*®. Copyright © 1973,
1978, 1984 by International Bible Society. Used by permission
of Zondervan. All rights reserved. Scripture quotations marked
KJV are taken from the King James Version of the Bible. (Public
Domain); and TLB are taken from *The Living Bible*, © 1971, Tyndale
House Publishers, Wheaton, IL 60189. Used by permission.

LCCN 2009907120
ISBN 978-1-4347-6480-5
eISBN 978-1-4347-0249-4

© 2009 Richard Exley
First edition published by Honor Books in 1991
© Richard Exley, ISBN 978-1-56292-116-3

The Team: Melanie Larson, Sarah Schultz, Jack Campbell, Karen Athen
Cover Design: Amy Kiechlin
Cover Photo: iStockphoto

Printed in the United States of America
Second Edition 2009

3 4 5 6 7 8 9 10

051510

*To all those men and women who,
in their grief, taught me not only
how to grieve, but how to find the
comfort of God*

CONTENTS

NOTE TO THE READER

I wrote *When You Lose Someone You Love* while serving as the senior pastor of a local congregation. At the time, I desperately needed a scripturally sound and practical book to give to grieving people. Not a book about grief—there were a number of those available, and not an autobiographical account of one person's grief—but a book that would speak directly to the grieving person, addressing the questions that person was dealing with as he or she walked through the valley of the shadow of death.

Having ministered to a number of grieving people during my twenty-five years in the pastorate, I knew how much energy it took to grieve; therefore the book had to be small. It also had to be real, honestly addressing the gut-wrenching issues death brings, especially the death of a child or the sudden and unexpected death of a spouse. And it had to be personal without being invasive, as well as scripturally sound but not preachy.

Although I found a number of excellent books, many of which are referenced in the notes and bibliography, I couldn't find exactly what I was looking for. Finally, I decided to take a stab at writing my own. With a proposal and a sample chapter in hand I approached my publisher. After some discussion they offered me a contract and I went to work.

I decided to make this book a series of letters addressed to a grieving person named "David." As you might suspect, David is not a real person; rather he is a composite of all the grieving people I have worked with. In order to protect their privacy, I have changed their names, and, in some instances, altered specific details regarding their loss. However, the reality of their grief and the concerns it gave birth to have been preserved as accurately as my memory affords. And because the individuals from whom this composite was constructed are real, the questions David raises and the issues he deals with in regard to the death of his beloved are also real.

I chose the letter style because it affords me the opportunity to speak to you directly and in a very personal manner. Although you and I have never met, I feel like I know you because we have walked in the same places. I have stood beside you as you laid your stillborn child to rest. I have held you in my arms as you wailed in anguish after learning your only child was killed by a drunk driver. I have watched in amazement as you have swallowed your own grief in order to comfort your children following the death of their father. I have admired your courage and the strength of your faith as you prepared to face the future without your spouse. In some small way, I have shared your pain and therefore I feel I can speak into your life.

I have no easy answers, no glib assurances, and I won't pretend that I know what you are feeling. I may have some idea, having walked this way with others who have experienced a loss similar to your own, but that is all—just an idea. Still, it is a place to begin, and if you will allow me to speak to you from the pages of this book, I believe the Lord will comfort you. Nothing I have written will take your pain away—only God can do that—but it will help you understand what you are experiencing and how to get through it.

I won't lie to you. There will be times when the pain will be nearly more than you can bear, but God will be with you and He will sustain you. He may not take the pain away, but He will give you the strength to bear it. And as great as your grief is, God's grace is greater still.

One final thing: The Lord is no respecter of persons (Acts 10:34 KJV), and what He has done for other grieving people He will do for you. Having witnessed His grace firsthand, I can assure you that no matter how much you are suffering, God will see you through, for He is the "Father of compassion and the God of all comfort, who comforts us in all our troubles" (2 Corinthians 1:3–4).

—Richard Exley

Then the end will come, when
(Christ) hands over the kingdom
to God the Father after he has
destroyed all dominion, authority
and power. For he must reign
until he has put all his enemies
under his feet. The last enemy
to be destroyed is death.

—1 Corinthians 15:24–26

When Death Comes

The first letter

Dear David,

How often I think of the loss of your beloved and the anguished grief to which it gave birth. The initial moments have been indelibly imprinted upon my mind. I can still see you smiling bravely as you rose to greet me when I came to give what comfort I could. Somehow that brave smile was even more heartrending than the sobs that came later. Even in the moment of your loss, you still wanted to be the caregiver; you wanted to make my task easier.

In your grief, you said that you felt handicapped, that you had never had to deal with anything like this before. How right you are. Nothing in life really prepares us for the death of a loved one, especially if that death is totally unexpected. Although we know that people—even children—die every day, we never think it can happen in our family. And with good reason, for it has been estimated that the average person can go through a twenty-year period without being exposed to the death of a single relative or friend.

Still, sooner or later all of us are confronted with the

inevitable. It may come unexpectedly. A phone call in the middle of the night notifies us of our brother's sudden death. A uniformed police officer quietly informs us of a fatal car accident involving our son or daughter. Or it may come as the long-awaited blow at the end of a lengthy illness. However it happens, it is always painful and inevitably followed by grief and an almost overwhelming sense of loss.

I won't pretend that I know entirely what you are feeling or that I can fully comprehend the depth of your grief. Nor will I pretend that I have all the answers to your tormenting questions. In truth, all I really have to share is my love and the painful lessons I have learned while dealing with my own grief and while helping others deal with theirs.

My first experience with death came when I was just nine years old. Mother was taken to the hospital sometime in the middle of the night, and Grandma Exley came to stay with my two brothers and me. For the next two and a half days, Mother struggled to give birth to her fourth child. She succeeded only after the doctors belatedly performed a cesarean section. I was too young to understand any of this, but I can remember the laughter and cheers when Grandma told us that we had a baby sister. In minutes we were announcing it to the neighborhood.

Sometime later, Dad came home and gathered us three boys around him. He was bowed with weariness and grief. With great difficulty, he told us the painful news. Yes, Mother had given birth to a daughter, our long-awaited sister, but things didn't look good. The baby was hydrocephalic and wasn't expected to live. Even if she did live, she would never be normal.

Tears were running down Dad's cheeks when he finished, and I seemed to be smothering. I couldn't get my breath. I sat there numbly for a minute; then I burst off the couch and ran through the dining room and kitchen, choking on my sobs. I flung open the screen door, making a frightful racket, and stumbled down the back steps toward the garage.

For the better part of the next hour, I lay facedown on the dirt floor. Great heaving sobs convulsed my small frame, and it seemed like everything in the universe withdrew, leaving me alone with my pain. The dusty floor mingled with my tears, becoming mud, and I pounded my fists into the ground until I had no strength left. After a long while, my grief seemed to exhaust itself, leaving me with a hollow feeling in the pit of my stomach.

I think I accepted Carolyn's death that afternoon, but it wouldn't become a reality until just before Christmas, three months later. The intervening weeks were filled with several crises. Once, Dad and Aunt Elsie rushed to the children's hospital in Denver. When they arrived, Carolyn was critical, at the point of death. The doctors were able to stabilize her condition, and after she had spent several days in the hospital, they brought her home for the last time. I vaguely remember Mother placing Carolyn in my lap as I sat in the armchair. She watched with a painful love as I fed my baby sister a few ounces of formula.

It seemed that each day brought some new disappointment. Soon we realized that Carolyn was both blind and deaf, and her head, larger than the rest of her tiny body at birth, became increasingly disproportionate. With a pain that still lingers, I remember watching Mother as she bathed Carolyn tenderly, then carefully measured her head to see if, by some miracle, it was any smaller. It never was. Mama would bite her lip, and silent tears ran down her cheeks as she put away the cloth tape measure.

Carolyn died in her sleep at home early one morning. Our family doctor and Aunt Elsie arrived at about the same time. He confirmed the death, and Aunt Elsie fixed breakfast, which no one ate. A short time later, the mortician came and took Carolyn's tiny body away, and the gray December day passed in a maze of necessary activities.

The funeral service and the trip to the cemetery have been completely blocked from my memory, leaving me without a single detail. However, I do remember eating supper after the funeral. Grief rendered the food tasteless, but we ate anyway, mechanically, out of some misbegotten sense of obligation. We ate in the kitchen with one small lamp as the only light. It cast deep shadows around the table, shadows that matched the sorrow in our hearts. To this day, I have not had a sadder meal.

As a child, I was able to accept Carolyn's death without affixing responsibility. It was enough to know that she was with Jesus, in heaven, where there is no more sickness or pain, no more sorrow or crying. By Christmas her death was already becoming a painful but fading memory.

The questions came later, after I became a pastor and found myself ministering to families in similar situations. Their desperate questions gave birth to my own: Was God to blame for Carolyn's death? Did He kill her, or at least allow her to die? Questions like these drove me to my knees. Desperately I searched the Scriptures for understanding.

After months of painful agonizing, I concluded that sin, not God, is responsible for disease and death. That is not to say that Carolyn's death was the result of her own personal sin, or even—God forbid—the sin of her parents. Rather, it means that sin has tainted the entire human race, and diseases and death are the inevitable consequences. Romans 5:12 (KJV) declares, "Wherefore, as by one man sin entered into the world, and death by sin; and so death passed upon all men."

As I counsel those who question why humans must suffer, sometimes I simplistically explain that we inhabit a planet which is in rebellion, that we are part of a race living outside of God's will, and that one consequence of that rebellion is sickness and death. God doesn't send this plague upon people, nor does He will it. It is simply a natural consequence of humanity's fallen state. Although as believers we are new creations in Christ (2 Corinthians 5:17), we remain a part of this human family—a family that is tainted by sin and death. As a consequence, we, too, suffer the inevitable repercussions of that fallen state, even though we may be personally committed to the doing of God's will and the coming of His kingdom.

In truth, the cause of sickness and death is not God but the hated enemy, sin. Not necessarily our personal sin, nor a specific sin—for life and death cannot be reduced to a mathematical equation—but the fact of sin.

Jesus addressed the relationship between personal sin

and death in Luke 13:1–5: "Now there were some present at that time who told Jesus about the Galileans whose blood Pilate had mixed with their sacrifices. Jesus answered, 'Do you think that these Galileans were worse sinners than all the other Galileans because they suffered this way? I tell you, no! Or those eighteen who died when the tower in Siloam fell on them—do you think they were more guilty than all the others living in Jerusalem? I tell you no!'"

Jesus does not tell us why these particular individuals died while others equally sinful were allowed to live, but He does make it clear that the reason for their deaths is far more complicated than mere cause and effect.

As you well know, David, when death strikes unexpectedly, we long for a reason, an explanation, but often there is none. In desperation we try to make some sense out of it, but often there are simply no pat answers, no ready conclusions. In times like these we must always resist the temptation to speak where God has not spoken. Beyond the simple explanation that death comes as a result of humanity's sinful state, God has not given us any insight into the "why" of individual deaths.

In many ways, David, death remains a mystery, even to the Christian. Why is one child taken in infancy and not another? Why is a good man stricken in the prime of life, leaving behind a wife and children, while other vicious and cruel men live to a ripe old age? Why? Why? Why? The questions are almost endless, and I must admit that I am often without answers, but of this one thing I am sure— God is not to blame! In fact, when tragedy strikes, when a loved one dies, God's heart is the first of all hearts to break!

In His comfort,
Richard

Lord Jesus, my grief is unspeakable; the pain never goes away day or night. I can't sleep. It seems I watch the clock tick away the minutes all night long. I have no appetite, no interest in food. The tastiest meal is tasteless in my mouth. All the color has gone out of my world, leaving it bleak and barren. Worst of all are the tormenting questions. Why did this happen? Why didn't You answer our prayers? Where are You when I need You?

Yet even in the darkest night I cling to You. I trust Your love and wisdom even when I cannot understand Your ways. In my heart of hearts, I know You are too wise to ever make a mistake and too loving to ever cause one of Your own needless pain. When I weep, I choose to believe that You are weeping with me. Knowing that You share my grief gives me comfort even if it doesn't take away the pain. The promise of Your presence and the hope of eternal life give me the strength to go on. With Your help I truly believe that my mourning will one day be turned into dancing, and until that happens, I will trust You. In Your holy name I pray. Amen.

Who shall separate us from the love
of Christ? Shall trouble or hardship or
persecution or famine or nakedness or
danger or sword? ... No, in all these things
we are more than conquerors through
him who loved us. For I am convinced
that neither death nor life, neither angels
nor demons, neither the present nor the
future, nor any powers, neither height nor
depth, nor anything else in all creation,
will be able to separate us from the love
of God that is in Christ Jesus our Lord.

—Romans 8:35, 37–39

Without Warning

The second letter

Dear David,

In my first letter I talked about the unspeakable pain of losing someone we love and the inevitable questions that always accompany their death. Although I did not address your situation directly, I hope and pray that you found the universal truths about God's faithfulness and compassion helpful. For my part I am strengthened, somehow, when I know that God shares my pain. The knowledge of His nearness does not render my grief painless, but it does give me the strength to bear it.

"Death," as Joe Bayly so aptly put it, "is a wound to the living."[1] Yet, like all wounds, some deaths are more severe than others. For instance, the death of a child is more painful than that of an aged parent. And an unexpected death is almost always more traumatic than one that comes at the conclusion of a lengthy illness.

Having served as a pastor for more than twenty-five years, I have had numerous occasions to walk with families through "the valley of the shadow of death." I have wept with parents following the accidental death of a beloved son. I have held the hand of a grieving widow as she tried to imagine life without her husband of nearly fifty years. And I have stood beside a tiny grave with a grief-stricken couple as they laid their stillborn child to rest. Although each experience of death is unique in its own way, in another sense, all grief experiences have many things in common.

I'd like to tell you about a particularly tragic experience because I think it may help you to better understand your own grief. It involves the unexpected death of a twenty-three-year-old woman, following a brief illness. Her family had no warning and no time to prepare for their tragic loss. In that sense their experience is not unlike your own, and, like you, they were left reeling. One minute they were a happy family, and the next moment their world was shattered.

Sherry's fatal illness began innocently enough one evening with a headache that grew more severe as the night progressed. Twice she telephoned her sister Corrie, who prayed with her and told her to try and get some sleep.

Later, after the extent of the illness had become known, Corrie told me that she had considered getting up and going to her sister's apartment but had decided against it. Sherry, she had reasoned, was a registered nurse and was fully capable of taking care of herself. Besides, it was probably just a migraine headache—extremely painful but not dangerous.

There were no more calls that night, and Corrie awoke in the morning feeling somewhat the worse for wear, but relieved. Routinely she prepared breakfast and got her girls off to school. By midmorning her house was straightened and she thought of calling her sister, but decided against it. Sherry, she reasoned, had probably had a rough night and was undoubtedly getting some much-needed rest.

When Sherry hadn't telephoned by noon, Corrie decided to go by her apartment and see how she was feeling. After ringing the doorbell several times without getting a response, she used her key to let herself in. Anxiously she called, "Sherry?" When there was no answer, her anxiety deepened. Moving into the bedroom, she noticed that the bed was unmade but empty. Then she heard soft moans coming from the bathroom where she discovered Sherry, on the floor, unconscious.

Rushing to her side, she tried to revive her, but to no avail. Quickly she dialed 911 and requested an ambulance. While waiting for the paramedics to arrive, she called her husband who, in turn, called me. I arrived at the hospital just minutes after the ambulance and spent the next hours trying to comfort the family while the doctors performed a battery of tests on the still-unconscious Sherry.

Several hours later, the doctor came in looking grim. "The diagnosis is not good," he explained to Corrie. "Your sister has spinal meningitis and is in a coma. We are moving her upstairs into ICU. If her condition continues to deteriorate, we will have to place her on a life-support system."

Corrie collapsed in her husband's arms and sobbed for several minutes. With a seemingly determined effort, she got hold of herself and took charge. Phone calls were made to family and friends, locally and across the nation. As word of the crisis spread, Christian friends began coming to the hospital to offer comfort and encouragement. Within hours the family arrived from out of state, and the vigil was underway.

For the next two and one-half days, we virtually lived at the hospital. Exhausting hours were spent in the intensive-care waiting room, interrupted only by brief visits to Sherry's bedside. Her room was deathly quiet, the only sound the soft whoosh of the breathing machine. Occasionally her mother or Corrie would kneel by the bed to pray or softly plead with her to get well, but all to no avail. Her condition remained unchanged.

Slowly, reality began to sink in. Sherry was not going to recover apart from a miracle. With that knowledge, our prayers took on a new urgency, then a certain desperation, and finally a painful resignation. Then the inevitable moment came. After consultation with the doctors, a decision was reached. There was no reason to continue to pretend that Sherry was alive. In truth, she was already dead. There was absolutely no trace of brain activity, and there hadn't been for two days. The medical staff disconnected the life-support system, and the family struggled to accept the unacceptable.

Life continued, but with a certain surrealism. The tragic truth was simply too painful to be comprehended, just as it was too real to be denied. A healthy twenty-three-year-old woman doesn't just suddenly contract a deadly disease and die. Not in America, not with all of the advances made by medical science. Yet Sherry had, and she had died. While her body was being prepared for burial, her stunned loved ones tearfully planned the funeral.

As atypical as Sherry's death was, the grief experienced by her loved ones was not unlike that which follows every death. As you may well recall from your own experience, David, bereavement is first encountered as a shock that some-how numbs the pain. You feel as if you have been swathed in great bands of cotton. You continue to comprehend reality and interact with the world, but as if from a great distance. Life goes on, but in slow motion. Everything seems to be filtered through layers and layers of insulation.

You can probably remember how the first two or three days passed in a maze of necessary details, which served to distance you from the reality of the death even as you seemed to be dealing with it. The details themselves were a sort of mandatory escape, a legitimate way of postponing the full force of your grief.

Every decision took on a special significance: What should your beloved be buried in? Who should you ask to give the eulogy? What Scriptures should be read, and who should conduct the service? Should you have the service in the funeral home or in the church? Should it be held in the morning or afternoon? What about special music? Should you accept flowers or establish a memorial fund? Who should pick out the casket and the burial plot? The list went on and on.

David, now that you are a few weeks removed from the loss of your beloved, can you step back from your pain and get a glimpse of the whole picture? Can you see how compassionate God is? Due to humanity's sinfulness, He cannot totally eradicate death, but He can and does make it somehow bearable. The shock we experience initially is His way of helping us deal with the pain of our loss. It works like a divine tranquilizer that enables us to comprehend the reality of death without feeling the full depth of our devastating loss. As the initial shock wears off, the promise of eternal life with our departed loved one becomes the gift of hope that keeps us going until grief has done its healing work.

After the funeral, life returns to something akin to normal for most of your family and friends, but not for you. For you, grief's long journey is just beginning. Long after the last casserole has been devoured and the serving dishes washed and returned, long after the last of your out-of-town relatives have said their good-byes and made the long journey home, long after your most caring friends have recovered from their grief and resumed a normal life, you still grieve. The pain of your loss lingers like a stubborn toothache.

And now, more than ever, you need the ministry of comfort. Not covered dishes and sympathy cards, but a safe place with a safe person, somewhere you can grieve without being rebuked or misunderstood. You need someone who will let you be real, someone who will let you weep or rage as the case may be, someone who won't try to explain the unexplainable, or fix everything with a prayer.

In my next letter, David, we'll talk about the healing power of grief. Until then, know that you are loved and that the things you are feeling are normal for someone who has lost a loved one.

One final suggestion: Don't let anyone make you feel guilty because you are still grieving. Grief is a slow process and often takes as long as two years to complete its healing work. That doesn't mean that you will always hurt this badly, but it does mean that you should give yourself permission to take as much time as you need to work through your loss.

In His comfort,
Richard

◇─────────────────────────────────────◇

Lord Jesus, I'm so tired. Even when I sleep, I don't rest. I toss and turn all night long, troubled by fitful dreams. I feel numb every waking moment. The things that once brought me such joy now leave me unmoved. Nothing seems to matter anymore and I can't help asking, "What good is life if I have no one to share it with?" Truthfully, it feels as if my life has been reduced to a prison of pain in which my only emotion is grief. Yet, even in the midst of my grief, I know that You are near. I can't always sense Your presence, but I know You haven't forsaken me. With Your help I will get through this. One day life will have meaning again. I know it will. Help me not to waste this painful time. Let me learn from it so at some future time I can comfort others who will be experiencing their own grief. In Your holy name I pray. Amen.

There is a time for everything,
and a season for every activity
under heaven: a time to be born
and a time to die ... a time to
weep and a time to laugh, a time
to mourn and a time to dance.

—Ecclesiastes 3:1–2, 4

The Truth About Grief

The third letter

Dear David,

By now you undoubtedly know more about grief than you ever wanted to know. You don't necessarily understand it, but you've experienced it. You know about the desolation of a hauntingly empty house that, not so long ago, resounded to the joyous laughter of your beloved. You know about eating alone at the table in the sunlit breakfast nook where the two of you so often enjoyed the quiet of early morning and talked of growing old together. You told me that you are painfully reminded of your aloneness and loss each time something—a few bars of a favorite song, a phone call from a friend, an old snapshot—reminds you of a shared experience. Only now you have no one with whom to share your feelings.

Following the death of his beloved wife, Davy, Sheldon Vanauken wrote,

> Along with the emptiness which is what I mean by loss, and along with the grief—loss and grief are not

the same thing—I kept wanting to tell her about it. We always told each other—that was what sharing was—and now this huge thing was happening to me, and I couldn't tell her.… I sometimes thought I could bear the loss and grief if only I could tell her about it.[1]

I remember another grieving widower telling me that the hardest thing for him to bear was when something interesting or funny happened and he would think, *I must remember to tell this to Margaret.* Then he would be reminded that Margaret had passed on. At such times his grief was nearly unbearable.

Because grief is so painful, you have probably been tempted to seek not only relief, but also escape. Don't! While that reaction is not unusual, it is counterproductive. As painful as your grief is, it is not a foe to be overcome but a friend to be embraced. If you insist on thinking of your grief as an enemy, you will only delay the healing process. You may deny your grief, even repress it for a time, but you cannot escape it. One way or another, you will grieve. The only real choice you have is how and when.

Grief itself is painful but not injurious. It is a wound that brings healing in much the same way a proper surgical procedure wounds the body in order to heal it. As C. S.

Lewis wrote in a letter to a dear friend whose wife had died,

> I am sure it is never sadness—a proper, straight natural response to loss—that does people harm, but all the other things, all the resentment, dismay, doubt and self-pity with which it is usually complicated.[2]

In the final analysis, David, grief is a healing gift from God. Jesus said, "Blessed are those who mourn, for they will be comforted" (Matthew 5:4). That promise is fulfilled when you grieve. When you weep, God weeps with you as surely as Jesus wept with Mary following the death of her brother Lazarus. And as you share your sorrow with God, you will experience His comfort and He will bear a portion of your grief. As the prophet wrote so long ago: "Surely he took up our infirmities and carried our sorrows" (Isaiah 53:4).

There are those who teach that Christians should not grieve. They falsely reason that since our loved ones have gone to be with the Lord, we should only rejoice and not weep. Don't be misled, David. The Scriptures teach otherwise. The apostle Paul tells us, "Rejoice with those who rejoice; mourn with those who mourn" (Romans 12:15).

And the writer of Ecclesiastes declares,

> There is a time for everything, and
> a season for every activity under heaven …
> a time to weep and a time to laugh,
> a time to mourn and a time to dance.
>
> —Ecclesiastes 3:1, 4

David, now is the time for you to mourn.

Paul, the foremost apologist for the resurrection, affirms both the promise of eternal life, which gives us hope in the dark hour of our loss, and the reality of death, which makes grief mandatory. In his first letter to the believers in Thessalonica, he encourages them to grieve but not in the same way that the world grieves. He writes,

> Brothers, we do not want you to be ignorant about those who fall asleep, or to grieve like the rest of men, who have no hope. We believe that Jesus died and rose again and so we believe that God will bring with Jesus those who have fallen asleep in him…. He died for us so that, whether we are awake or asleep, we may live together with him.
>
> —1 Thessalonians 4:13–14; 5:10

David, without God, death is an unequivocal tragedy, but seen in the light of our Lord's resurrection, it is reduced to a wound to the living. Of course, this knowledge does not eliminate your pain and loss, but it does put it into perspective. You still grieve, but not with the disconsolate grief of those who have no hope of life beyond this world.

As I write these words, I can almost see you nodding, as if you want to reassure me, but with a pained and faraway look in your eyes. It's the same look I've seen from time to time as you've hinted at a crisis of faith. You've never quite put it into words, but I believe I have sensed it. If I'm reading something into your words that isn't there, please forgive me. On the other hand, if indeed you are experiencing dark times, times when your sorrow is so deep you find yourself questioning the very existence of God (or at least His goodness), then I want to encourage you. And, if possible, I would like to walk with you through your "dark night of the soul."

You are not the first person who has found himself doubting the very things that he once held most sacred and dear. In fact, such doubt is almost inevitably a part of great grief. That doesn't make your desolation any less painful, but hopefully it does make it less frightening. Sometimes just knowing that other people have gone this way before can be enormously encouraging, especially if you know they made it through successfully.

I was helped in my own journey by a little book titled *Tracks of a Fellow Struggler*. It was written by a Baptist minister named John Claypool. It details his personal battle with unbelief as he walked through "the valley of the shadow of death" with his ten-year-old daughter, who was fighting a losing battle with leukemia. Like all grieving persons, he fought a battle of his own, a battle he describes with moving candor:

> I perhaps need to confess to you that at times in the last few months I have been tempted to conclude that our whole existence is utterly absurd. More than once I looked radical doubt full in the face and honestly wondered if all our talk about love and purpose and a fatherly God were not simply a veil of fantasy that we pathetic humans had projected against the void.... There were the times, for example, when Laura Lue was hurting so intensely that she had to bite on a rag and used to beg me to pray to God to take away that awful pain. I would kneel down beside her bed and pray with

all the faith and conviction of my soul, and nothing would happen except the pain continuing to rage on. Or again, that same negative conclusion tempted when she asked me in the dark of the night: "When will this leukemia go away?" I answered: "I don't know, darling, but we are doing everything we know to make that happen." Then she said: "Have you asked God when it will go away?" And I said: "Yes, you have heard me pray to Him many times." But she persisted: "What did He say? When did He say it would go away?" And I had to admit to myself He had not said a word! I had done a lot of talking and praying and pleading, but the response of the heavens had been silenced.[3]

In moments like that, Claypool was tempted to conclude that God, if He existed at all, was either cruel or incompetent. But he resisted that temptation. Instead, he clung tenaciously to the conviction that God was good and merciful, even though the pain of his present circumstance seemed to indicate otherwise. By an act of his will, he chose to believe that there is more to life than meets the eye. Like Paul, he came to grips with the fact that "for now we see through a glass, darkly" (1 Corinthians 13:12 KJV).

Quite frequently we feel ashamed of our grief, especially when we feel angry at God. Somewhere we have picked up the mistaken idea that such feelings reveal something negative about our faith. Nothing could be further from the truth. David, the intensity of your grief does not indict your faith. Rather, it testifies to the depth of your love and the richness of the relationship you enjoyed with your beloved.

In another sense, the honest acknowledgment of your most real feelings may very well say something about the quality of your faith—not something negative either, but something positive! It takes tremendous trust to bare your heart and soul to God when it requires you to express disappointment, doubt, and anger. Somewhere we have picked up the idea that these are not the kinds of emotions a "true" Christian should have. Still, for those who are grieving, such feelings are real, and in order to work through them, they must honestly share them with God. It's their only hope. Denial is nothing more than a slow death.

Perhaps my words seem blasphemous, as if I am tempting you to commit a sacrilege. Not so! God already knows what is in your heart, so what can be gained by pretending? There is a certain risk, to be sure, in expressing your doubts and unbelief, not to mention your anger. After all, you might get stuck there. Still, it is the only way. You must trust God to help you work through your feelings.

I am encouraged when I remember that in the hour of His death Jesus experienced the same kind of haunting questions that torment us, yet without being guilty of sin (Hebrews 4:15). He, too, felt that God had forsaken Him: "And at the ninth hour Jesus cried out in a loud voice, *'Eloi, Eloi, lama sabachthani?'*—which means, 'My God, my God, why have you forsaken me?'" (Mark 15:34).

But Jesus did not allow Himself to become trapped there. Having honestly expressed His soul's deepest despair, He was able to move from that tormenting question to an affirmation of His faith: "'Father, into your hands I commit my spirit.' When he had said this, he breathed his last" (Luke 23:46).

Although His circumstances were obviously different from yours, I think there is a truth to be learned. You cannot get beyond your doubts and fears until you honestly face them in God's presence. Having done that, you are free to reaffirm your faith and recommit yourself to the God of all grace!

Of course, that doesn't mean that you are finished with your grief—but that's a letter for another day. It does, however, signal progress. You have moved into a new dimension, a new honesty in your relationship with God. Now you can walk through "the valley of the shadow of death"—not without pain, but without despair, for you do not walk alone.

In His comfort,
Richard

◇────────────────────────────────◇

Lord Jesus, I love You, but I'm really angry right now. I don't want to feel this way, but I can't seem to help myself. The doctors did everything they could, but in the end they were powerless. I did everything I was capable of doing and still my beloved died. Had I done any less I would have never been able to forgive myself. You are the only one who did nothing, or so it seems to me. You have the power of life and death and yet You did not intervene. You could have healed her but You didn't. You could have prevented the accident but You didn't. All of us, who have such limited power, did everything we could, but it feels like You, who have all power, did nothing at all. I'm trying to understand why You didn't do anything, but right now I can't.

Hurt and anger are making me bitter, killing the relationship we once shared. I want to punish You, yet even in my anger I know You are my only hope. With one hand I push You away while with the other hand I cling to You with all my might. With a trembling faith I lift my hurt to You, trusting that You will take it from me. Replace my anger with acceptance, I pray, and my hurt with hope. I ask not for understanding, for I know I will never understand why things happened the way they did, but for trust. Give me unconditional trust that I may rest in You no matter how grievous my loss. In Your holy name I pray. Amen.

Praise be to the God and Father
of our Lord Jesus Christ, the
Father of compassion and
the God of all comfort, who
comforts us in all our troubles.

—2 Corinthians 1:3–4

The Tides of Grief

The fourth letter

Dear David,

In your last letter, you said that just about the time you thought things were starting to get back to "normal," you were suddenly overwhelmed with a fresh wave of grief. You went on to say that when that happened, you felt your loss as acutely as in the days immediately following the funeral. Then you asked, "When will this terrible pain end?"

I wish I knew, but I don't. As I mentioned in an earlier letter, grieving is a lengthy process and often requires two or three years to complete its healing work. Of course, you will not always grieve with the same intensity; no one could bear that. Gradually you will find that the awful edge of your grief is lessening. You will experience a renewed interest in life. It won't happen all at once, and there will be numerous reversals when you are caught once again in the painful throes of mourning. Still, as the seasons pass, you will experience a springtime in your life as the long winter of your grief draws to a close. One of the best ways to understand what is happening is found in the analogy you used, "a fresh wave of grief."

In truth, grieving is a lot like the tide; it comes in waves. Immediately following the death of a loved one, we are overwhelmed with a sense of loss and the accompanying sadness. The tide of grief comes rushing in, but we are protected from the enormity of our loss by shock, by the all-consuming details surrounding the death and burial, and by the comforting presence of family and friends. However, once the funeral is over and life returns to its familiar routine, we experience a great weariness and an unspeakable sadness.

Although this is an overwhelmingly difficult time, it is not unexpected. You were prepared for it; that is, as much as anyone can prepare for something like this. With determination you suffered through those first few weeks. There were moments of rage, moments when you were incensed by the injustice of it all, and moments when you were tempted to blame God. At other times I know you were unbearably sad. There were even periods of depression when you were tempted to isolate yourself. Still, little by little the awful edge of your grief dulled. Then, you said, you still hurt, but it was less a searing pain and more a stubborn ache.

Then came the day, at last, when you seemed to awaken from the long night of your grief. It would be going too far to say that you were happy, but at least you were not unhappy, not sad.

For the first time since that fateful moment when you learned of her death, you felt like your old self. (Remember when you called just to tell me how good you were feeling?) You concluded, incorrectly, that you were over your grief. In truth, what you were experiencing that day is similar to what people who are sick feel when they finally turn the corner following a lengthy illness. The sky suddenly seems bluer, the sun brighter, and a zest for living returns, but there will still be many days of recuperation before they fully recover.

In *A Grief Observed,* C. S. Lewis says,

> There are moments, most unexpectedly, when something inside me tries to assure me that I don't really mind so much, not so very much, after all. Love is not the whole of a man's life. I was happy before I ever met H. I've plenty of what are called "resources." People get over these things. Come, I shan't do so badly.... Then comes a sudden jab of red-hot memory and all this "commonsense" vanishes like an ant in the mouth of a furnace.[1]

I believe that pretty well sums up what is happening to you. Following a brief period when you seemed relatively free of grief, you suddenly find yourself grieving again. To use your analogy, when you finally thought you were beginning to regain your emotional equilibrium, you were blindsided by a fresh wave of grief.

Now, once again, you find yourself weeping at the oddest moments. Your melancholy has returned and you've lost all interest in life. People weary you, and yet you cannot bear the thought of being alone. You find it difficult to follow or respond to their casual conversation; it seems so uninteresting. Nevertheless, you want people around, if only they would talk to each other and not you.

This is a pattern that will repeat itself again and again over the next several months. The tides of grief will come in and go out. You will experience times of intense grief followed by periods of relative calm. Then the tide will come in again, and once more you will grieve. Just as suddenly, the tide will go out again so that, if you did not know better, you would think you were finally over your grief. Of course, you're not. This is just another "resting period" before you resume your "grief work."

As grief does its healing work, you will begin to notice some subtle changes. When the tide of grief rolls in, it will not come in quite as far, nor will it stay as long. And when it rolls back, it will go out further and stay out longer. Your times of grief will become briefer and less intense, while your times of rest will become longer and more renewing.

Another subtle change is in the way you think about your beloved. In the initial stages of grief, almost all of your thoughts are filled with loss. As you well know, you cannot think of your beloved without remembering her terrible suffering and the depressing details of her death. The funeral service and the trip to the cemetery are still haunting memories. You brood about what might have been or what should have been. No memory of her is free from pain.

By and by those painful memories will be replaced by earlier ones when you shared the joy of life, reminiscences of happier times when death seemed nothing more than a distant possibility. But the first few times you remember her without experiencing grief's familiar pangs, you will undoubtedly feel guilty, as if you have betrayed her memory. You may find it helpful to remember that as it is unhealthy to repress grief when you experience it, even so it is also unhealthy to manufacture sorrow when it is not there. Those who grieve in a healthy manner accept their feelings as valid, whether sorrow or comfort, and offer them to God in worship.

Another reason you may long to hold onto your sorrow is

because it may seem to be all you have left of the life you shared together. In the book *Song for Sarah*, a grieving mother says,

> My feelings are the only thing I have left which hasn't been wrested from me. My tears and my pain over you are all I still have which belongs to the three of us. Everything else is gone. So even if it does hurt, it's the last thing I have which is ours. Everything else in my life is new—you can see that. These tears are all that's left of us.[2]

In truth, the redemptive work of grief is intended to heal your broken heart so you can remember your beloved without always reliving the pain of her death. Her death may have been the last thing you shared, but it is not the only thing. You also shared her life, and I want to encourage you to allow the God of all comfort to balance those last painful memories with the early joyous ones. I'm not suggesting that you attempt to block out the memory of her death, but only that you make it a part of the integrated whole. As difficult as it may be, you must remember the life she lived and the times you had together.

In His comfort,
Richard

Lord Jesus, I want to thank You for never leaving me alone in my grief. Without the strength of Your presence I don't think I could have made it. Now that my terrible pain is easing a little, I realize that You were with me even when I was sure You were nowhere to be found. I want to thank You for allowing me to vent, to honestly express my feelings, even the ones I know I shouldn't have had. Thank You for being patient with me, for giving me time to work through my feelings. Today is a "good" day and for that I give You thanks. A day like this makes me believe that there may even be life after my beloved's death; no matter how much I miss her or how deeply I grieve. I give You praise this day and every day. In Your holy name I pray. Amen.

When you pass through the waters, I will be with you; and when you pass through the rivers, they will not sweep over you. When you walk through the fire, you will not be burned; the flames will not set you ablaze. For I am the Lord, your God, the Holy One of Israel, your Savior.

—Isaiah 43:2–3

The Pitfalls of Grief

The fifth letter

Dear David,

As you well know, grief is an inevitable part of our human condition. Sooner or later all of us experience the death of someone we love, and with it, the pain of grief. Yet for all of grief's familiarity, few of us are really prepared for it. As a consequence, we risk not only our future happiness, but our emotional wholeness as well.

During the grieving process you must avoid two temptations, either of which can be emotionally crippling. The first is the temptation to pretend that you are fully recovered when you're not. As you have undoubtedly discovered, most people are uncomfortable with grief. As long as you are visibly grieving, they may avoid you if they can. Since all of us need acceptance, especially in times of grief and loss, it is natural to hide your grief in order to be accepted. This may seem to work for a time, but in actuality it only delays the healing process.

The rejection you may be experiencing is not personal, although it certainly feels very personal. Being rejected is common to all who have experienced great grief. For instance, following his wife's death, C. S. Lewis noted,

> An odd by-product of my loss is that I'm aware of being an embarrassment to everyone I meet. At work, at the club, in the street, I see people, as they approach me, trying to make up their minds whether they'll "say something about it" or not…. Some [chunk] it altogether. R. has been avoiding me for a week.[1]

Lewis concludes, somewhat tongue-in-cheek I think,

> Perhaps the bereaved ought to be isolated in special settlements like lepers.[2]

Most people who seem to avoid you probably do so because they simply don't know what to say, nor do they understand the comfort a compassionate listener affords the grieving person. The naked reality of our loss and the intense emotions it has birthed are likely frightening to them. The questions raised, the pain you share, may well strike too close to home, threatening their own carefully constructed worldview. Most people are simply not ready—or able—to deal with their own doubts, let alone yours. Whatever the reason, you must not allow their negative reactions to cause you to repress your honest grief in order to avoid rejection.

The second temptation is to wallow in your grief. I'm not suggesting that you deny the reality of your loss in order to appear recovered, but I know that grief has a fatal fascination for most of us. There is something "tragic," even "romantic," about those who have suffered a great loss, especially if they seem to suffer nobly. If we are not careful, "bearing our grief" can become a pseudo badge of courage, the thing that sets us apart from all others. After a time it is easier to play the part of the grieving spouse or parent or child than it is to come to grips with our loss and get on with the business of living.

The most common way this second temptation manifests itself is through an abnormal and unhealthy preoccupation with grief. While it is normal to be consumed with our loss in the initial stages of grief, past a certain point it becomes counterproductive. Healthy grief may require months (even as much as two years or more) to complete its work, but it is not static. It moves from a sense of loss to one of grateful appreciation. That is to say, as grief does its healing work, the way we think about the departed will change.

Initially, all we can remember is our beloved's sickness and death, but after a while we begin to recall the life we shared together. This change doesn't come about all at once, nor is it final. Little by little we find ourselves remembering the good times we experienced with one another. These positive memories will be interspersed with painful episodes when the memory of their death returns with frightening clarity. Still, as time goes on, more and more of our thoughts will be of the life they lived rather than the death they died. That's the healing power of grief.

Although grief's work cannot be hurried, there are certain things we can do to facilitate it. Let me illustrate. Some years ago I was working with a mother who was mourning the accidental death of her sixteen-year-old son. When she came to see me, several months had passed, but the full impact of his death was just beginning to sink in. With great sorrow she told me of the funeral and the trip to the cemetery. The day had been cold and rainy, and she said it had broken her heart to leave her "little boy" alone in that kind of weather. In fact, she had returned to the cemetery that night, where she had stood at his grave for more than an hour, oblivious to the inclement weather. Having told me that, she hastened to assure me that she knew her son wasn't really in that casket, that his spirit was with God, but …

There, in my presence, she began to come to grips with the terrible truth of her son's death. For the first time she dared to put her true feelings into words. Finally she felt safe enough to vent all the grief she had so carefully concealed. All she could think about was what he had missed. He never had a date or owned his own car. He never graduated from high school, never went to his senior prom. He never attended college, married, or had children of his own. Her list was endless, and in great sorrow she poured out the agony of her soul.

After several sessions, I felt that the time had come for us to move on, so I gently suggested that she spend some time each day remembering the good times she had shared with her son. In order to make the memories specific, I asked her to put them in the form of a letter to her departed son. Finally, I asked her to conclude each letter with a prayer.

My purpose was really very simple. By asking her to remember the good times they had shared, I was encouraging her to recall not just her son's death, but his life as well. Of course, this did not nullify his tragic death, but it did serve to put it into the context of the life he had lived. As long as she had those special memories, her son would never be far from her thoughts. And by asking her to conclude each letter with a prayer, I was making it possible for her to give to God both her grief and her gratitude.

A few days later she wrote,

> Dear Son,
>
> Today is such a beautiful day. The sun is shining and the leaves are blowing under the trees.
>
> Remember when we went to Elephant Rock State Park? You climbed on the big rocks and said, "Look, Mom, I am king of the mountain." When it was time to go I said, "Come on, Froggie," and the boys next to you said, "Froggie? What a funny name for a kid." We laughed all the way home.
>
> You were four years old then and I guess that was the day you got your nickname. You never seemed to mind that I called you Froggie all these years. I love you very much.
>
> Always,
> Mom

She concluded with a prayer:

Dear God!

Thank You for the sun and the trees. Thank You for the laughter that only children can bring in their special way. Please, Lord, help me to heal my heart and spirit so I can be a light for You.

As the weeks went by, she began to recover. Little by little her good days began to outnumber her bad days. Eventually her memories of her beloved son became a source of comfort rather than searing pangs of grief. Now when she thinks of him, her first thoughts are usually of some childhood prank or of some tender, poignant moment, rather than of his fatal accident. Of course, there will always be those times—his birthday or the anniversary of his death—when she will experience again the pain of her loss. But for the most part she is now able to thank God for the sixteen years she and her son had together, rather than blaming Him for his premature death.

David, I shared all of this with you because it may be time for you to take control of your grief. For the most part it has been controlling you these past few months—and that's okay. But if you hope to get beyond this point, you will have to take some responsibility for your recovery. Maybe the

time has come for you to change your focus. Heretofore you
have mourned your loss. Perhaps now it is time for you to
give thanks for the years you and your beloved had together,
thanks for the richness of the life you shared.

In an earlier letter I referred to a book titled *Tracks
of a Fellow Struggler* in which John Claypool discusses his
struggle to make some sense out of the death of his ten-year-
old daughter. He concludes,

> I have two alternatives: dwelling on the fact that she
> has been taken away, I can dissolve in remorse that
> all of this is gone forever, or, focusing on the wonder
> that she was given to us at all, I can learn to be grate-
> ful that we shared life, even for an all-too-short ten
> years.… The way of remorse does not alter the stark
> reality one whit and only makes matters worse. The
> way of gratitude does not alleviate the pain, but it
> somehow puts some light around the darkness and
> builds strength to begin to move on.[3]

David, your beloved was a gift from God, pure and
simple. She was never really yours, not in the sense that we
tend to think. You were privileged to enjoy life with her for

a time, and now she is gone. You can hold that fact against God and grow bitter, or you can thank God you were given the gift of her presence for a time, however short.

If you choose to thank God for what you had, rather than to mourn what you have lost, I believe you will discover a new dimension of life. That doesn't mean you won't grieve or that you won't miss her. Rather, it means that not even death can rob you of the joys you shared together! Nor can it steal your present hope or the promise of the future. The God who makes all things new is now present to renew your life. He wants to give you the grace to enjoy living again!

In His comfort!
Richard

Lord Jesus, replace my grief with gratefulness. Help me to remember the life we shared rather than just the death she died. Replace the painful memories of her suffering with the joyous memories of our life together. Help me to remember the first time I saw her and the way she smiled at me from across the room. Let me remember our wedding day, the births of our children, and the many times we prayed together, lifting our concerns to You with thanksgiving. Let me remember her zest for living, her devotion to our family and friends, and most of all her remarkable faith. These are gifts not even death can take from me. In Your holy name I pray. Amen.

I took you from the ends of the earth,
from its farthest corners I called you.
I said, "You are my servant";
I have chosen you and have not rejected you.
So do not fear, for I am with you;
do not be dismayed, for I am your God.
I will strengthen you and help you;
I will uphold you with my righteous right hand....
For I am the LORD, your God,
who takes hold of your right hand
and says to you, Do not fear;
I will help you.

—Isaiah 41:9–10, 13

The Promise of His Presence

Dear David,

As a minister, I have often shared the grief of those whom the Lord has entrusted to my care. Although that has been a tragically sad responsibility at times, it has also afforded me the opportunity to witness not only the faithfulness of God, but also the faith of His people and the strength faith provides, especially in the hour of our greatest loss.

Not even those who have great faith, however, endure grief without questions. Inevitably their concerns have a common theme. Although each person expresses his apprehension in his own unique way, it can generally be summed up in two or three common questions.

First, the bereaved want to know if God has forsaken them, if He has abandoned them in the dark hour of their grief. The emptiness they experience and the desolation they feel often make it seem that He has. Second, they want to be assured that God knows what they are experiencing and that He cares. Finally, they ask, "Can God bring something good out of this terrible experience?"

As you well know, David, one of the things that makes the death of a loved one so difficult is that we often feel that God has forsaken us. Of course, He hasn't, but there are times when it feels as if He has. Such feelings are common to those who grieve, and there is no reason to be ashamed of them. Even C. S. Lewis, the great Christian apologist, struggled with feelings of abandonment following his wife's death. Of that experience he wrote,

> Meanwhile, where is God? This is one of the most disquieting symptoms. When you are happy, so happy that you have no sense of needing Him, so happy that you are tempted to feel His claims upon you as an interruption, if you remember yourself and turn to Him with gratitude and praise, you will be—or so it feels—welcomed with open arms. But go to Him when your need is desperate, when all other help is vain, and what do you find? A door slammed in your face, and a sound of bolting and double bolting on the inside. After that, silence. You may as well turn away. The longer you wait, the more emphatic the silence will become. There are no lights in the windows. It might be an empty house. Was it

> ever inhabited? It seemed so once. And that seeming
> was as strong as this. What can this mean? Why is
> He so present a commander in our time of prosperity
> and so very absent a help in time of trouble?[1]

In times like that, we must remember that while our feelings are real, they are not necessarily accurate. That is to say, it truly feels as if God has deserted us, that He has left us alone with our grief. He hasn't, but it feels as though He has. Through the centuries, spiritual pilgrims have referred to this sense of abandonment as "the dark night of the soul." They triumphed in those dark times by choosing to trust in the truth of God's Word rather than the raging of their emotions.

The Scriptures contain many promises of His abiding presence. Promises like Deuteronomy 31:8 declare, "The LORD himself goes before you and will be with you; he will never leave you nor forsake you. Do not be afraid; do not be discouraged."

The last thing Jesus did before ascending into heaven was to give His disciples the promise of His presence. "And surely I am with you always, to the very end of the age" (Matthew 28:20).

These promises and countless others like them are a source of tremendous strength when you are grieving. Yet, what has helped me the most in my hour of desolation is a passage from Isaiah 49:

> For the LORD comforts his people and will have
>   compassion on his afflicted ones.
> But Zion said, "The LORD has forsaken me, the Lord
>   has forgotten me."
> "Can a mother forget the baby at her breast and
>   have no compassion on the child she has borne?
>   Though she may forget, I will not forget you!
> "See, I have engraved you on the palms of my
>   hands."
>
> —Isaiah 49:13–16

Can a mother forget the child she has conceived? Can she forget that joyous moment when she first felt that new life move within her womb? Can she forget the hours she spent praying and dreaming about their life together? Can she forget the moment of birth, when she went to the very doorway of death to bring forth life, when at last the awful agony of labor was forgotten in the delirious joy of holding her tiny child for the very first time? Can she forget the infant that nursed at her breast? Can she forget?

I cannot imagine how she could, but God says, "Though she may forget, I will not forget you!" In other words, the only thing worthy to be compared with God's love for us is a mother's love for her child. Yet, even that special love pales in comparison with God's eternal and unconditional love for His children. As unimaginable as it may seem, there are mothers who abandon their own children, but God will never forsake one of His own!

In the hour of grief—no, I should say in the weeks and months of grief—when it seems there will never be an end to our grieving, when it seems all of life is one sad song, we still have a choice. We can choose to believe what seems to be the truth—God is absent. Or we can ignore the visible evidence in favor of the invisible reality. We can choose to believe that God is present and that one day soon our shaken emotions will once again recognize His nearness.

Many times the pain of our loss blinds us to the reality of God's presence. Only later when we look back and review the days of our grief do we realize that He was with us all the time, even when we were sure He was nowhere to be found. As Henri Nouwen points out in *The Genesee Diary,*

> What is most close, most intimate, most present, often cannot be experienced directly but only with a certain distance.... Only in retrospect do I realize that something very important has taken place. Isn't this true of all really important events in life? When I am together with someone I love very much, we seldom talk about our relationship. The relationship, in fact, is too central to be a subject of talk. But later, after we have separated and write letters, we realize how much it all meant to us, and we even write about it.[2]

Isn't this what happened to the grieving disciples on the road to Emmaus? Jesus spent an entire day with them, even expounded the Scriptures to them, and yet they did not recognize Him. Only later, when He had disappeared from their sight, did they begin to reflect on their experience. Then they said, "Were not our hearts burning within us while he talked with us on the road and opened the Scriptures to us?" (Luke 24:32).

At other times God manifests His presence indirectly, through other people. Paul writes, "When we came into Macedonia, this body of ours had no rest, but we were harassed at every turn—conflicts on the outside, fears within. But God, who comforts the downcast, comforted us by the coming of Titus" (2 Corinthians 7:5–6).

Remember the lady I wrote about whose teenaged son died in a tragic accident? One morning when she was feeling particularly low (or to use her words, "really in the pits"), her doorbell rang. She wrestled momentarily with the idea of ignoring it. Her eyes were red from crying, her hair was a mess, and she was still in her robe. It rang again, and she forced herself toward the front door.

The caller was a friend from church, and when Joyce opened the door, the friend breezed right in, announcing, "I've come to talk with you." Noticing Joyce's disheveled appearance, she quickly added, "And if you don't feel like talking, I'll just sit with you, and if you want to cry," she continued, brandishing a box of tissues, "I'm prepared to cry with you."

By this time they were back in the kitchen where the uninvited guest proceeded to rummage around until she found the coffeemaker and got it going. The two friends spent the rest of the morning over coffee laced with conversation and tears. As they talked, the strangest thing happened—Joyce began to feel better. She was still sad, but now she was no longer alone with her sadness. A friend was present and shared her sorrow. And in some mysterious way God was present too, and He comforted her.

When Joyce related that incident to me, she concluded very wistfully, "If only there were more people like her. And she brought her own tissues! Can you believe that?"

Think for a moment, David. How many times over these past weeks and months has someone been there for you? Oh, I know the many times we have failed you: the long evenings you've spent alone, the meals taken by yourself, the telephone that never rang. Still, think of the times you have been comforted in your grief by a phone call that came at "just the right time." Coincidence? Hardly. And what about the cards and letters, the notes that seemed to come with an inspiring word just when you were on the verge of giving up. Was that just a coincidence? I don't think so.

Maybe Alexander Irvine expressed it best in his novel *My Lady of the Chimney Corner.* Irvine has "the lady" go comfort a neighbor whose boy lay dead:

> As gently as falls an autumn leaf, she laid her hand on
> Eliza's head: "Ah, woman, God isn't a printed book to
> be carried aroun' by a man in fine clothes, not a cross

danglin' at the watch chain of a priest. God takes a hand whenever He can find it and does what He likes with it. Sometimes He takes a Bishop's hand and lays it on a child's head in benediction, and then He takes the hand of a doctor to relieve pain, the hand of a mother to guide a child, and sometimes He takes the hand of a poor old craither like me to give comfort to a neighbor. But they're all hands touched by His Spirit, and His Spirit is everywhere lukin' for hands to use."[3]

Remember, David, the hand that brings you comfort and encouragement is always God's hand, and He is never far from His own.

In His comfort,
Richard

Lord Jesus, forgive me. I have been so consumed with my grief that I have been blind to all the ways You have come to me—in the presence of my pastor, a phone call from a dear friend, a dinner invitation when I couldn't bear to eat alone again, and in the laughter of my grandchildren. At the time these things seemed no more than ordinary events, but I now realize that You were present in each and every one, bringing me comfort in that moment and hope for the future. Truly it is Your hand that comforts and encourages me. Help me to remember that You are never far from me no matter how alone I feel. In Your holy name I pray. Amen.

I have told you these things,
so that in me you may have
peace. In this world you will
have trouble. But take heart! I
have overcome the world.

—John 16:33

The Depth of His Love

The seventh letter

Dear David,

Again and again these past weeks you have asked, "Does God know what's happening to me? Does He care?" At other times you have wondered, "Why didn't He do something to prevent this awful tragedy?"

I've given considerable thought to your questions, and I am convinced that it's not really answers you seek as much as assurance. Intuitively you know that suffering and death are often shrouded in mystery, that there are simply no pat answers. Still, the nagging questions remain, replayed in your mind, over and over again. You long for some word, some explanation, that will restore your confidence. As it is, you are beset by a haunting uncertainty. Although you may never have put it into words, I sense that deep down you wonder if you can really trust God.

Don't be embarrassed: Your doubts are as old as mankind. In the midst of grief almost everyone is tempted to feel the way you do. Yet, at the same time you love God more intensely than you ever have. These feelings may seem contradictory to you, and you may even be tempted to wonder if you are losing your mind. You're not! Grief gives birth to a host of different emotions. The Lord understands this, and He comes to us in the midst of our emotional storms.

Following the unexpected death of their brother, Lazarus, Martha and Mary experienced an overwhelming grief, which gave birth to questions not unlike your own. Like you, they were troubled by the tragedy of losing a loved one, and they could not help but question our Lord's goodness.

"'Lord,' Martha said to Jesus, 'if you had been here, my brother would not have died'" (John 11:21). With those words she accused Jesus of failing, of not caring, of ignoring them in the hour of their greatest need. Does that sound familiar?

What did Jesus do? How did He respond? He absorbed her anger without rebuke. He understood how things must seem from her limited perspective, how much she loved her brother, and how deeply she hurt.

Yet, she didn't stop there. Like you, she still loved Jesus intensely and wanted to believe. Even in her anger, her faith expressed itself: "I know he will rise again in the resurrection at the last day.… I believe that you are the Christ, the Son of God, who was to come into the world" (John 11:24, 27).

When she quickly moved from anger to faith, Jesus met her there and built on her confession. He said to her, "'I am the resurrection and the life. He who believes in me will live, even though he dies; and whoever lives and believes in me will never die. Do you believe this?' 'Yes, Lord,' she told him" (John 11:25–27).

Mary responded differently. She, too, was hurt and angry, maybe more hurt and angry in keeping with her temperament:

> When Mary reached the place where Jesus was and saw him, she fell at his feet and said, "Lord, if you had been here, my brother would not have died." When Jesus saw her weeping … he was deeply moved in spirit and troubled.… [And] Jesus wept." (John 11:32–33, 35)

Notice that Jesus also met Mary where she was. And there was little or no faith in her confession beyond the faith to tell Jesus how she really felt. Somehow, even in her grief and disappointment, she believed He would understand, and He did. For her, He had no theological pronouncements, no revelation about resurrection life, no discourse about His divine sonship. Why? Not because these things were any less true then, but because Mary was not ready to receive them. There was nothing in her heart but sorrow and tears, so He met her at the place of her grief. He wept with her.

If Jesus came to Martha and Mary in the hour of their grief, will He not come to you? If He understood what they were feeling and shared their feelings, will He not do as much for you? How did I put it in my first letter? "When tragedy strikes, when a loved one dies, God's heart is the first of all hearts to break!"

I'm hesitant, David, to give you too many Scriptures because I know that the shock of grief can render the eternal Scriptures temporarily unreal. Yet, I also know that nothing comforts and illuminates like the Word of God, especially when it is spoken in season. Nothing so quiets the frightened heart, so stills the troubled soul, as the Holy Scriptures.

Think for a moment. Haven't there been times, especially of late, when the Scriptures have spoken to the deepest and most profound longings of your soul? Haven't you discovered new words of hope and encouragement in familiar verses, passages that you've known for years? Is this mere chance? Not on your life! It is God's way of manifesting Himself, His way of comforting you in the depths of your grief.

Your questions may still remain, but somehow they don't seem quite so important now. God has given you something better than understanding—trust, a trust that is rooted not in explanation but in the assurance that He cares.

Dr. David McKenna, president emeritus of Asbury Theological Seminary, tells of a friend who lost his daughter in a flash flood along the Big Thompson River in Colorado. He says,

> When I met him two weeks after the tragedy, his eyes were sunk in dark sockets from weeping. Awkwardly, I asked, "How is it going?"
>
> Never given to public testimony or eloquent statements, his sad eyes looked back, and he spoke almost from a trance, "The hurt goes deep, but His love goes deeper."[1]

That, David, is the essence of trust. No matter how deep your grief, God's love goes deeper still.

In His comfort,
Richard

Lord Jesus, thank You for absorbing my raging emotions, my angry accusations, and my explosive grief without rebuke. Had I not been able to express my honest feelings to You, they would have surely poisoned my spirit. Help me not to get stuck here. Help me to work through these turbulent emotions, to move from hurt and confusion to acceptance and finally to unconditional trust. Help me to rest in Your love and in the great promises of Scripture. In Your holy name I pray. Amen.

And we know that in all things
God works for the good of those
who love him, who have been
called according to his purpose....
What, then, shall we say in
response to this? If God is for
us, who can be against us?

—Romans 8:28, 31

If God Is for Us

The eighth letter

◇——————————————————————————◇

Dear David,

I couldn't agree with you more when you say that one of the things that makes death so difficult to accept is that it seems such a waste. As rational creatures, we find simply unbearable the thought that a fatal accident or illness might be pointless, of no eternal value. On the other hand, if we can be assured that God will ultimately bring good out of what looks for all the world like a senseless tragedy, then we can somehow endure it.

Given that hope, it is not uncommon for the bereaved to try to figure out how God is going to bring good out of their tragedy. It is a futile exercise for the most part, because God's ways are far beyond anything we could ever imagine. In fact, trying to discover His ultimate purpose while you are in the midst of grief often leads to absurd conclusions or to outright despair. Nevertheless, you may be assured that one day you will understand how God redeemed your terrible loss and caused it to work for eternal good.

I am not suggesting, not even for a moment, that God caused the death of your beloved, for He did not! In time you will come to see how He has turned what now seems nothing more than a senseless tragedy into a miracle of grace. The very thing that the Enemy intended to use to destroy your faith can become an instrument by which God furthers His eternal purpose in your life and in the kingdom. Just how He will do that, I don't know; but that He will do so, I am sure.

Many years ago, I heard about a minister whose son committed suicide. Ten days after the funeral, the minister stood at the pulpit and announced his text. Under real duress, he read Romans 8:28: "And we know that in all things God works for the good of those who love him, who have been called according to his purpose." Visibly struggling, he said,

> I cannot make my son's suicide fit into this passage. It's impossible for me to see how anything good can come out of it. Yet, I realize that I only see in part; I only know in part. The scope of this verse is beyond me; I can't comprehend it. Still, somehow it supports me, enables me to go on living even though life

doesn't seem to make any sense. Somehow I believe that when all of life is over, when God has fully worked out His perfect will, even my son's suicide will be woven into the final tapestry of His eternal design.

It's like the miracle of the shipyard. Almost every part of our great oceangoing vessels is made of steel. If you take any single part—be it a steel plate out of the hull or the huge rudder—and throw it into the ocean, it will sink. Steel doesn't float! But when the shipbuilders are finished, when the last plate has been riveted in place, when the last part has been bolted properly, then that massive ship is virtually unsinkable. By the design of the master shipbuilder, steel has been made to float!

Taken by itself, my son's suicide is senseless. Throw it into the sea of Romans 8:28, and it sinks. But I believe that when the Eternal Shipbuilder has finally finished, when God has worked out His perfect design, even this senseless tragedy will somehow work to our eternal good. I can't even imagine how, but I know it will!

David, you asked me what good can possibly come out of your beloved's death. I wish I could tell you, but I can't. All I can do is assure you that God is too wise ever to make a mistake. And He is too loving to ever allow one of His children to go through needless pain.

I see you struggling to make some sense of this tragic death, trying to see how it can possibly be made to fit into your understanding of God's perfect plan. I don't fault you for this, but I must counsel you to be careful. Death is not a riddle to be solved or a question to be answered; instead, it is a mystery to be entrusted to the wisdom of God.

Rather than trying to understand how God is going to bring good out of your beloved's death, it might be more beneficial to consider some historic examples of how He has redeemed other seemingly senseless tragedies. Quite frequently the good that God works can only be seen in retrospect. Even then we only see in part. We must wait until eternity to understand the full scope of His eternal craftsmanship.

On January 8, 1956, Jim Elliot and four other missionaries were brutally murdered by the Aucas, a savage tribe of manhunters living in the Ecuadorian jungles. At first glance, their deaths seemed like a tragic waste of life, especially Jim Elliot's. Not only was he a young husband and father, he was also a missionary of rare and special ability. Even as an undergraduate at Wheaton College, he had shown a remarkable spiritual maturity. His personal pilgrimage is chronicled in his diary (published posthumously as *The Journal of Jim Elliot*), which contains some of the most profound spiritual concepts recorded in the last century. His entire life was characterized by a burning passion to reach the unreached peoples of the world with the gospel of Jesus Christ. Just prior to his death, he completed a translation of the gospel of Luke for the Quechuas, a tribe of South American Indians.

In light of all of this, we are tempted to ask why God would allow such a gifted and dedicated young man to be martyred at the age of twenty-nine. His ministry was just beginning. Surely the kingdom could not afford the loss of one so able.

Upon further examination, however, we can see God working to redeem this tragedy. When news of the deaths of the five missionaries was announced in Christian schools, hundreds of young people volunteered to take their places. The story caused world missions to be front-page news in *Life* magazine and newspapers around the world.

Helen Roseveare, who served for many years in the

Belgian Congo as a missionary doctor with the Worldwide
Evangelism Crusade, shared a touching incident that further
shows how God brings good out of tragedy. She reports,

> A young missionary couple during their first term of
> service in a foreign land were expecting their first baby.
> The mother wrote me from the hospital a few days
> after the birth to tell me that her baby had died.…
> She went on in her letter, "Local women whom I've
> been trying to reach with the gospel visited me yes-
> terday, and their loving sympathy was very touching.
> Then one of them said to me, 'Now you are the same
> as us. Now we will listen to what you tell us.' I find
> my heart rising above my sorrow.… I can identify
> with the local community in their daily sufferings
> and so be able to share Christ with them."[1]

When Dale Evans Rogers lost her two-year-old daughter, Robin, she poured out her grief and her hope in the
beautiful book *Angel Unaware*. Because she was willing to
be honest and to allow God to use her loss, society's attitude
toward and treatment of children with Down Syndrome was
drastically changed.

Dr. Norman Vincent Peale wrote of Dale,

> She is a mother who has won great victory over great
> sorrow.... I saw at once that Robin, her baby, had not
> lived and died in vain. Where most babies die and leave
> the mother crushed, Robin put on immortality and
> her mother found the very joy of God in what might
> otherwise have been an overwhelming tragedy.[2]

Given these examples and many others like them, one might be tempted to conclude that God caused these deaths in order to advance the work of the gospel. I cannot believe that. God is not the author of death, but of life.

Death is the archenemy of God, a consequence of humanity's fallen state. It is a defeated enemy, to be sure, but it has not yet been destroyed:

> For he [Jesus] must reign until he has put all his ene-
> mies under his feet. The last enemy to be destroyed
> is death....
>
> Then the saying that is written will come true: "Death
> has been swallowed up in victory."

"Where, O death, is your victory?

Where, O death, is your sting?" The sting of
death is sin…. But thanks be to God! He gives us the
victory through our Lord Jesus Christ.

—1 Corinthians 15:25–26, 54–57

God uses death in the same way an expert in self-defense uses his opponent's weight and momentum against him. When death strikes, God takes that unspeakable loss and uses it as an opportunity to bring good out of evil.

Of course, David, I must admit that it is much easier for me to write about these truths than it is for you to live them. Although my heart hurts, my suffering is nothing compared to your grief. I can view these tragic events somewhat objectively; you cannot. In many ways I am an outside observer, while you are the central participant. As the main participant, you obviously know more about the devastation of death; but as a more objective observer, I probably have a better understanding of the big picture. And in order to make some sense of your loss, you must not insist on seeing it as an entity unique unto itself. You must come to the place where you can view it as a single piece of an integrated whole—a piece that finds its true meaning only in relationship to the eternal whole. Let me illustrate:

In June 1815 the English military forces under the Duke of Wellington engaged the forces of Napoleon Bonaparte. All England awaited news of the outcome. It was before the days of fast communication, and watchers were stationed along England's coast to observe the sailing vessels coming up the Channel. Any special news would be wigwagged by semaphore to those waiting.

Knowing the battle was to be fought, the coastal sentries waited for a message of its outcome. Finally a watcher noted a message being waved from a passing boat, "Wellington defeated…" And then the fog closed in. The words were relayed across England, and the nation was plunged into gloom.

When the fog cleared again, another sailor on another boat waved the same message—this time without interruption: "Wellington defeated the enemy." England's sorrow was banished and the entire country went wild with joy.[3]

In the befogging pain of grief, we are able to see only part of the message, and as a result, death often seems like the ultimate insult. It appears to be the final indignity that makes a mockery of our faith. But when the fog of grief begins to clear even just a little—when at last we are able to perceive the whole truth—it becomes obvious that death is a defeated enemy, one that God uses for His eternal purposes until He ultimately destroys it:

> Therefore we do not lose heart. Though outwardly we are wasting away, yet inwardly we are being renewed day by day. For our light and momentary troubles are achieving for us an eternal glory that far outweighs them all. So we fix our eyes not on what is seen, but on what is unseen. For what is seen is temporary, but what is unseen is eternal.
>
> —2 Corinthians 4:16–18

David, in closing let me say that I am not naive enough to think that anything I write can eliminate the painfulness of your grief. You do not lose someone you love dearly without experiencing the deepest sorrow of which the human heart is capable. I do believe, however, that the spiritual and emotional devastation caused by your grief can be minimized—no, more than that, redeemed—if you can be helped to see it in its eternal context. Once you have accomplished that feat, your grief will not necessarily be less, but it will become pain with a purpose. And history has shown us that humans can bear an almost unlimited amount of suffering if they can be assured that it will count for something.

Let me encourage you to offer your beloved's death, along with your grief and loss, as a gift to God. Give Him permission to use it any way He sees fit. Do this, and I truly believe that God will redeem it for His glory and your good.

In His comfort,
Richard

◇————————————————————————————————◇

Lord Jesus, I know that my beloved did not live in vain. Her life was rich with meaning, and she enriched everyone whose life she touched. I'm tempted to think of her death as a waste, an unspeakable loss, but by an act of my will I choose not to. Instead I choose to remember that You have a long history of bringing good out of the most unspeakable loss. Although I cannot imagine how, I choose to believe that You will bring eternal good out of this terrible tragedy. With a trembling heart I offer you a sacrifice of praise, lifting both my beloved's death and my painful grief to You in worship. Redeem her death and my grief. In Your holy name I pray. Amen.

Do not let your hearts be troubled.
Trust in God; trust also in me.
In my Father's house are many
rooms; if it were not so, I would
have told you. I am going there
to prepare a place for you. And
if I go and prepare a place for
you, I will come back and take
you to be with me that you
also may be where I am.

—John 14:1–3

BUSINESS REPLY MAIL

FIRST-CLASS MAIL   PERMIT NO. 560   FLAGLER BEACH FL

POSTAGE WILL BE PAID BY ADDRESSEE

THE QUILTER
PO BOX 422411
PALM COAST FL   32142-8235

In My Father's House

The ninth letter

Dear David,

As I look back over the correspondence we have shared these past months, I am struck by the fact that we have said so little about your beloved. Our letters have focused on what has been happening to you—your grief and your loss. To an uninitiated observer this might appear self-centered, even unfeeling, but it is neither. In truth, it is an affirmation of our belief in eternal life. We have not concerned ourselves with her present state because we are confident, as Paul says, that to be absent from the body is to be present with the Lord (2 Corinthians 5:8 KJV).

Having said that, however, I do think the time has come for us to address the question of life after death. This single issue, more than any other, distinguishes the way believers grieve from the way those without the hope of eternal life deal with death.

Until the very moment of death, David, all of your thoughts were for your beloved. You agonized as you watched her suffer, tormented by your own inability to do anything to relieve her pain. You seemed to die a little each day as you watched her grow weaker. Yet, when she breathed her last, your awful grief was tempered by the knowledge that she was home at last with the Lord of life. Her suffering was over. Never again would she writhe in pain.

Later when you wrote to thank me for being with you during her last days, you included a few words from a book I had sent you. Do you remember? You quoted from *A Severe Mercy* by Sheldon Vanauken:

> As I stood there in that suddenly empty room, I was suddenly swept with a tide of absolute knowing that Davy still was. I do not mean that I thought her body might still live; I knew it didn't. But past faith and belief, I knew quite overwhelmingly that she herself, her soul—still was.[1]

Then you wrote,

> Better than anything I might say, this passage describes what happened to me when she died. I knew, in a way I had never known anything before, that she was more alive than she had ever been. Even

during my darkest hours, when grief made my life
nearly unbearable, I never wished to bring her back,
not if it meant she would ever have to suffer again. I
have to admit, though, that I sometimes begged God
to take my life. For the first time, I think, I know
something of what Paul might have felt when he
wrote, "I desire to depart and be with Christ, which
is better by far" (Philippians 1:23).

When I read those words, David, I couldn't help thinking
that your confidence in your beloved's immortality was well
justified. Jesus said, "I am the resurrection and the life. He who
believes in me will live, even though he dies" (John 11:25).

Although none of us knows exactly what happens at
the moment of death, both Scripture and experience give us
every reason to believe that all is well.

When I was a young man in my first pastorate, I had
the honor of ministering to a wonderful Christian lady as
she faced death. She was suffering from terminal cancer, and
as she grew physically weaker, I could not help but notice
how her thoughts turned more and more toward heaven. As
the moment of her death drew near, she fixed her attention
on the opposite side of the room, and the most peaceful

expression settled on her countenance. Just before she drew her last breath, she said in a voice barely audible, "Jesus. I see Jesus."

Now if this were an isolated incident, it would be comforting, but not necessarily conclusive. But it is not an isolated incident. Scripture and experience combine to testify to the fact that there is life after death. Taken together, they constitute an impressive witness and continuing source of encouragement.

Stephen, the first Christian martyr, cried out as he was being stoned: "Look," he said, "I see heaven open and the Son of Man standing at the right hand of God" (Acts 7:56).

Billy Graham relates a similar testimony from his wife, Ruth:

> Ruth tells about an experience she had in China. On the station where she lived, one of the evangelistic missionaries was Ad Talbot, whom she affectionately called Uncle Ad. Talbot had five sons and a daughter, Margaret Gay, a girl he deeply loved. Sometime after her death he was in the country with a Chinese Christian woman who was dying. As he knelt beside her bed, the old woman's face lit up and she said to

> Uncle Ad, "I see heaven, and Jesus is on the right
> hand of God, and Margaret Gay is with him." At
> that moment the room was filled with heavenly
> music and the Chinese woman was dead.[2]

As you know, David, Christianity teaches that at the instant of death, our new life begins. The moment we take our final breath on earth, we take our first breath in heaven. Our bodies are placed in the grave to await the resurrection, but our spirits are immediately present with the Lord.

Dr. George C. Robinson, one-time professor of Old Testament studies at McCormick Theological Seminary, once remarked, "Most people dread death, but personally, I am not afraid to die, though I don't court death.... Christians face death with faith, believing that it opens the door to a land of goodness and gladness." Sudden death means sudden glory. Think of the thrill the believer will feel upon arriving home.

> Think of stepping on shore,
> And finding it heaven!
> Think of taking hold of a hand,
> And finding it God's hand!

> Think of breathing a new air
> And finding it celestial air!
> Of feeling invigorated,
> And finding it immortality!
> Of passing from storm and tempest into perfect calm!
> Of awaking and knowing—
> I am home![3]

When your beloved died, her spirit went immediately to be with the Lord. Even as you were making the painful preparations for her funeral, she was fully alive. Yet her redemption is not complete, and will not be, until she receives her glorified body at the second coming of Jesus Christ. Now she eagerly awaits the redemption of her body (Romans 8:23). Her burial, according to Scripture, was like the planting of a seed: "When you sow, you do not plant the body that will be, but just a seed.... The body that is sown is perishable, it is raised imperishable; it is sown in dishonor, it is raised in glory; it is sown in weakness, it is raised in power; it is sown a natural body, it is raised a spiritual body" (1 Corinthians 15:37, 42–44).

The question before us then is not, "Is there life after death?" That's a scriptural certainty! But rather, "What is the nature of that life?" What we want to know is, "How are the dead raised? With what kind of body will they come?" (1 Corinthians 15:35).

Most of our questions regarding the details of eternal life will probably go unanswered. The reality of our immortality is simply beyond us. We have no frame of reference and nothing to which we can compare it. Any earthly thing God might use as a way of comparison would diminish the glories of heaven at least as much as it revealed them. As a consequence, most attempts to describe heaven are little more than exercises in futility.

As you may remember, following Davy's death, Sheldon Vanauken wrote an essay speculating about the nature of their eternal life together and the activities in which they might be engaged in the hereafter. In the end he acknowledged that he had attempted the impossible: "Of course it will not be like that. What it will be is quite beyond anything we can imagine."[4]

Anyone who has ever seriously tried to describe this eternal realm knows something of his frustration. For instance, the apostle Paul wrote, "Fourteen years ago I was taken up to heaven for a visit. Don't ask me whether my body was there or just my spirit, for I don't know; only God can answer that. But anyway, there I was in paradise, and heard things so astounding that they are beyond a man's power to describe or put in words (and anyway I am not allowed to tell them to others)" (2 Corinthians 12:2–4 TLB).

Given that truth, perhaps the place to start is not with heaven, but with our glorified bodies. If we can come to some understanding of what they will be like, then maybe we can imagine, at least in some small way, the glories of heaven. Since our resurrected bodies will be fashioned after our Lord's glorious body, which is mentioned in Philippians 3:21, we need look no further than the risen Jesus to see what they will be like.

The first thing one notices about Jesus following His resurrection is that His appearance is so "human." Although He has a spiritual body, it is composed of flesh and bone. The disciples could see Him with their natural eyes, and they could touch Him with their natural hands. When He appeared to them following His resurrection, He said, "Look at my hands and my feet. It is I myself! Touch me and see; a ghost does not have flesh and bones, as you see I have" (Luke 24:39).

In fact, Jesus' appearance was so "ordinary" that on that first Easter morning, Mary Magdalene mistook Him for the gardener (John 20:10–16). And later that same day, two disillusioned disciples journeyed with Him from Jerusalem to Emmaus without recognizing Him. They thought He was just another weary traveler (Luke 24:13–35).

On more than one occasion after His resurrection, Jesus enjoyed a meal with His friends. The first time He appeared to His disciples, He asked them, "'Do you have anything here to eat?' They gave him a piece of broiled fish, and he took it and ate it in their presence" (Luke 24:41–43). On another occasion He surprised the weary disciples by preparing breakfast for them on the beach following a long night of fishing (John 21:1–14).

Yet, for all that, Jesus' resurrected body was no ordinary body. He was not limited by time or space but appeared and disappeared at will. He would suddenly materialize in the presence of those who believed in Him and just as suddenly disappear, only to reappear someplace else. In truth, His resurrected body had all the advantages of this natural body but none of its limitations. And since our mortal bodies will be transformed into the likeness of His glorious body, we, too, can expect to enjoy the same freedom from the limits of time and space.

I would like to think, David, that in heaven we will

be able to eat without getting fat; that we will be able to exercise without growing sore; that we will be able to work without becoming weary; that we will be able to love without being jealous or possessive; that we will be able to enjoy relationships without misunderstanding; that we will be able to worship fully and uninhibitedly; and that we will be able, finally, to know God completely—even as He knows us.

In heaven, singers will sing as they have never sung before. Composers will compose new music on a scale heretofore unknown. Creative geniuses will continue to invent. Gifted craftsmen will design and build things their natural minds couldn't even conceive. Writers will write and preachers will preach—but in that glorious realm everything will be done to a degree never imagined by mortal man.

Now look what I've done. I've allowed myself to be drawn into the very trap I was determined to avoid—using earthly comparisons in an attempt to describe heaven's eternal glories. It simply will not work! How did Vanauken put it? "Of course it will not be like that. What it will be is quite beyond anything we can imagine."[5]

And so it will: "No eye has seen, no ear has heard, no mind has conceived what God has prepared for those who love him" (1 Corinthians 2:9).

David, although we cannot conceive of heaven's glories, the promise of eternal life nonetheless provides an undeniable strength in the time of loss, as well as an unwavering hope for the future. It does not eliminate the pain of our grief, but it does put it into perspective. Let me illustrate.

Some years ago my brother and his family left the United States to become missionaries in Argentina. For them, it was the fulfillment of a lifelong dream. For the rest of us it was a painfully blessed moment. We were happy for Don and his family. He had prepared his entire life for this moment. We knew that he would be happier in Argentina, that this work was what he was destined to do. Still, we were nearly overwhelmed with our grief. All we could think about were the thousands of miles that would separate us, the four years we would be apart. Try as we might, we could not hold back our tears.

With a determined effort, we reminded ourselves that this separation, painful though it was, was only temporary. All of us would be reunited in the not-too-distant future. Without question, that was a comfort to us as we said our good-byes, but it did not fill the emptiness we felt as Don and his family boarded that huge 747, nor did it stop our tears. Yet, even as we cried, we were also rejoicing.

That's how believers grieve when a loved one dies. We are not without hope; nor are we fatalistic, as those who have no assurance of eternal life are; but still there are tears, for death creates a great void in the lives of those who are left behind. In truth, we celebrate eternal life with a tear in our eye.

For departed believers, death is not the end of life; rather, it is simply the end of sin, sorrow, and suffering. Their lives continue, and your beloved's life continues, on a scale we cannot imagine: "And I heard a loud voice from the throne saying, 'Now the dwelling of God is with men, and he will live with them. They will be his people, and God himself will be with them and be their God. He will wipe every tear from their eyes. There will be no more death or mourning or crying or pain, for the old order of things has passed away'" (Revelation 21:3-4).

David, we both know that your beloved is with Jesus. She is more alive now than she has ever been. Still, that does not mean that you should not grieve. Yet, even in the midst of your grief, you can find comfort in the promise of an eternal reunion. In eternity you will be reunited with your beloved; you will renew your relationship on a higher level than any you ever experienced here.

I say that based on what both Scripture and reason reveal about life after death. Although the ultimate reality of heaven is beyond our comprehension, God has revealed the essence of it. And always that essence is of a far grander scale than anything this earthly life affords. That being the case, how can we doubt that our most intimate earthly relationships will not be enhanced in heaven? I agree with C. S. Lewis, who said, "I think the union between the risen spouses will be as close as that between the soul and its own risen body."[6]

David, take hope. The best is yet to come!

In His comfort!
Richard

Lord Jesus, You are the resurrection and the life! You have conquered death, hell, and the grave. You have prepared an eternal abode for Your own and already my beloved is with You. Her suffering is over. You have wiped the last tear from her eye, and she is more alive than she has ever been. Although my loneliness is unspeakable, I would not bring her back for anything. As much as I love her, I know You love her more. As happy as she was with me, I know she is even happier being with You. I take strength from Your abiding presence and comfort from Your promise of eternal life. One day my beloved and I will be together with You forever. Life without end! May Your name be glorified now and forever. Amen.

EPILOGUE

TELLING DADDY GOOD-BYE[1]

◇————————————————————————————◇

In November 2006, my eighty-three-year-old father fell and broke his hip. Subsequently, he underwent surgery and several weeks of rehabilitation before being released to our care. My sister turned the office in her home into a sick room, and all of us children chipped in to purchase a queen-size adjustable bed so Mother could continue to sleep with Daddy.

This was just the latest in a series of health crises that had beset my father. For twenty-two years he had battled heart disease—undergoing two open-heart surgeries—and fibrosis of the lungs. With a tenacity born of love and desperation, my mother and my sister took Dad from one doctor to another, always hoping for a magical cure. While the doctors were sympathetic, there wasn't really anything they could do except try to make Dad as comfortable as possible. In time he seemed to make peace with his situation, finding joy in reading and playing table games with Mother, but it wasn't much of a way to live. On more than one occasion he told me that if it wasn't for leaving Mom, he would welcome death. He wasn't being morbid; he was simply tired of suffering and homesick for heaven.

By the new year it had become apparent that Dad was dying, although neither my sister nor my mother could bring herself to admit it. The thought of losing him was simply more than they could bear. In late January, the doctors confirmed what we could no longer deny, telling us that our father had only two to four weeks to live. When my sister broke the news to Dad, a small smile touched his lips, and he said, "Well, they've finally given me some good news."

Soon all the children, grandchildren, and even the great-grandchildren gathered at my sister's home in Texas, and on Thursday afternoon, February 8, 2007, my father departed this world. His homegoing was peaceful, although the weeks preceding it were filled with considerable suffering. He bore it all with remarkable grace—the pain and choking, the inability to eat and the humiliation of not being able to care for himself. As the end drew near, he became ever more affectionate, repeatedly kissing and hugging those of us who cared for him.

The last Sunday before his death we all crowded around his bed for worship. For the most part Dad seemed oblivious, but when it came time to receive Communion, he opened his eyes and reached for the cup and the bread. Kneeling beside his bed, I took his hand and began to quote John 14:2–3 (KJV). As I said the familiar words, "In my Father's house are many mansions …" he moved his lips, soundlessly mouthing the words along with me. As we sang his favorite hymns, he seemed to draw strength from them. Not strength to live but the strength to pass from this life to the next without fear.

Two days later he fell into a coma from which he awakened only momentarily at the very end. Mother was lying on the bed beside him, as was my sister. My brothers were at his bedside: Bob was standing at the head of the bed, softly stroking Daddy's hair, while Don was standing beside him, holding Daddy's hand. Standing between them and just a little behind, I had a clear view of my father's face. For days he had lain with his head back and his mouth wide open as he labored to breathe, but as he drew his last breath, he closed his mouth and opened his eyes. Focusing on something only he could see, Daddy smiled and tried to sit up, and then he was gone.

Thinking about it now, I am sure Jesus came for Dad just as He promised He would: "If I go and prepare a place for you, I will come again, and receive you unto myself; that where I am, there ye may be also" (John 14:3 KJV). There was no death angel in that room, just the Lord of life coming to call my father to his eternal reward.

The images of the last days I spent with my father have been forever etched upon my heart. One of the many things I will never forget is the memory of the love and devotion heaped upon him by his family and friends. It was a rare and special thing, and I can only conclude that the man or woman who goes into eternity loved like that is rich indeed.

The funeral service was deeply moving, filled with memories of the past and hope for the future. No one captured the hope of eternal life more powerfully than my brother Don. Having spent nearly all of his adult life serving as a missionary in Latin America, he understands what it means to be a pilgrim and a stranger in a foreign land. When it was his turn to speak, he said, "For the past thirty years I have been required to carry official documents identifying me as a 'resident alien.' Although I drink *mate* like an Argentine, eat *asado* with the best of them, and speak the language as if it were my mother tongue, I am still a 'resident alien,' and I always will be. I love Argentina and its people, but I will never be an Argentine. I am an American, and America will always be my home."

Pausing to collect himself he continued, "When we went to the mission field in 1976, we were truly cut off from our families and our homeland. There was no satellite television or Internet, and it took weeks to arrange an international telephone call, not to mention the prohibitive expense. After four long years we flew home for our first furlough. When we landed at Miami International Airport, I spotted a U.S. Postal Service drop box and began to weep. I know that must seem silly to you, but it symbolized home to me, and I was overcome with emotion. In the ensuing years we have passed through customs scores of times upon our return to the United States; still each time we do, Melba eagerly waits for the immigration official to stamp her passport and then look up and say, 'Welcome home.'"

Struggling to control his emotions, he said, "When Daddy took his last breath, I knew I had lost an irretrievable part of myself. The man who gave me life was gone, and it felt like I had a hole in my heart. On another level, I rejoiced because I knew Daddy was more alive than he had ever been, and even as I wept with grief, I rejoiced for him. With the eye of faith I saw Daddy getting his passport stamped at heaven's gate. I could almost hear Jesus say, 'Welcome home, Dick Exley! Welcome home.'"

It gives me great joy to recall Don's words, and more especially to know that Dad is no longer a "resident alien" in this world of pain, but a full-fledged citizen of heaven and a member of that great cloud of witnesses (Hebrews 12:1). Of course, this does not eliminate the pain of our loss, but it does put it into perspective. Even as we grieve, we are comforted with the knowledge that one day we will be reunited never to part.

Good-bye, Daddy. I will always love you. In life you taught me how to live, and in death you have shown me how to die with dignity. Your fingerprints are all over my life, and I will always be in your debt.

NOTES

Letter 2

1. Joe Bayly, quoted in H. Norman Wright, *Training Christians to Counsel* (Denver, CO: Christian Marriage Enrichment, 1977), 133.

Letter 3

1. Sheldon Vanauken, *A Severe Mercy* (New York: Harper & Row, 1977), 180–81.

2. C. S. Lewis, quoted in Vanauken, *A Severe Mercy,* 183.

3. John Claypool, *Tracks of a Fellow Struggler* (Waco, TX: Word, 1974), 77.

Letter 4

1. C. S. Lewis, *A Grief Observed* (New York: Seabury, Crossroad, 1961), 7–8.

2. Paula D'Arcy, *Song for Sarah* (Wheaton, IL: Harold Shaw, 1979), 76.

Letter 5

1. Lewis, *A Grief Observed,* 12.

2. Ibid., 13.

3. Claypool, *Tracks of a Fellow Struggler,* 82–83.

Letter 6

1. Lewis, *A Grief Observed,* 9.

2. Henri J. Nouwen, *The Genesee Diary* (New York: Image, 1981), 140–41.

3. Alexander Irvine, *My Lady of the Chimney Corner,* quoted in Maxie Dunnam, *Barefoot Days of the Soul* (Waco, TX: Word, 1975), 114–15.

Letter 7
1. David L. McKenna, *The Jesus Model* (Waco, TX: Word, 1977), 41.

Letter 8
1. Helen Roseveare, "The Spirit's Enablement," quoted in John W. Alexander, ed., *Confessing Christ as Lord: The Urbana '81 Compendium* (Downers Grove, IL: InterVarsity, 1982), 170.

2. Norman Vincent Peale, quoted in Joyce Landorf, *Mourning Song* (Old Tappan, NJ: Fleming H. Revell, 1974), 156–57.

3. Richard E. Orchard, "Our Magnificent Hope" *Advance Magazine*, April 1968, 4.

Letter 9
1. Vanauken, *A Severe Mercy,* 176.

2. Billy Graham, *Facing Death and the Life After* (Waco, TX: Word, 1987), 239–40.

3. Herbert Lockyer, *The Funeral Sourcebook* (Grand Rapids, MI: Zondervan, 1967), 183.

4. Vanauken, *A Severe Mercy,* 176.

5. Ibid.

6. C. S. Lewis, quoted in Vanauken, *A Severe Mercy,* 205.

Epilogue
1. A version of this first appeared in Richard Exley, *From Grief to Gratefulness* (Tulsa, OK: Vallew, 2008), 111–18.

BIBLIOGRAPHY

Alexander, John W., ed. *Confessing Christ as Lord: The Urbana '81 Compendium.* Downers Grove, IL: InterVarsity, 1982.

Benson, Bob, and Michael W. Benson. *Disciplines for the Inner Life.* Waco, TX: Word Books, 1985.

Claypool, John. *Tracks of a Fellow Struggler.* Waco, TX: Word, 1974.

D'Arcy, Paula. *Song for Sarah.* Wheaton, IL: Harold Shaw, 1979.

Dunnam, Maxie. *Barefoot Days of the Soul.* Waco, TX: Word, 1975.

Elliot, Elisabeth. *Shadow of the Almighty.* New York: Harper & Row, 1958.

Graham, Billy. *Facing Death and the Life After.* Waco, TX: Word, 1987.

Landorf, Joyce. *Mourning Song.* Old Tappan, NJ: Fleming H. Revell, 1974.

Lewis, C. S. *A Grief Observed.* New York: Seabury, Crossroad, 1961.

Lockyer, Herbert. *The Funeral Sourcebook.* Grand Rapids, MI: Zondervan, 1967.

McKenna, David L. *The Jesus Model.* Waco, TX: Word, 1977.

Nouwen, Henri J. *The Genesee Diary.* New York: Image, 1981.

Orchard, Richard E. "Our Magnificent Hope." *Advance Magazine*, Volume 4, Number 4, April 1968.

Shibley, David, and Naomi Shibley. *The Smoke of a Thousand Villages.* Nashville, TN: Thomas Nelson, 1989.

Vanauken, Sheldon. *A Severe Mercy.* New York: Harper & Row, 1977.

Wright, H. Norman. *Training Christians to Counsel.* Denver, CO: Christian Marriage Enrichment, 1977.

ABOUT THE AUTHOR

Richard Exley is the author of thirty-two books, most recently *Intimate Moments for Couples* and *From Grief to Gratefulness. The Making of a Man* was a finalist for the prestigious Gold Medallion Award. Known as a master storyteller, Richard uses his gift with consummate skill in *The Alabaster Cross,* his first novel. Richard's articles have appeared in numerous magazines including *Leadership Journal, Charisma, Ministries Today, The Pentecostal Evangel, Advance Magazine, Enrichment,* and *New Man.* His rich and diversified background has included serving as senior pastor of churches in Colorado and Oklahoma as well as hosting several popular radio programs, including the nationally syndicated *Straight from the Heart.*

Much in demand as a guest on both radio and television, Richard has appeared on the *700 Club, Richard Roberts Live, Action Sixty, The PTL Club, The New Jim Bakker Show, The Harvest Show,* and a host of other local television and radio programs. When not traveling the country as a speaker, Richard and his wife, Brenda Starr, spend their time in a secluded cabin overlooking picturesque Beaver Lake in northwest Arkansas. Richard enjoys quiet talks with old friends, kerosene lamps, good books, a warm fire when the weather is cold, and a good cup of coffee any time. He's an avid Denver Broncos fan, an aspiring bass fisherman, and an amateur photographer. Please visit the author and check out his podcasts at www.RichardExleyMinistries.org.